Getting Away

To Get It Together

Getting Away To Get It Together

A GETAWAY GUIDE
FOR COUPLES

Bill and Carolyn Wellons

FAMILYLIFE
Publishing™

Little Rock, Arkansas

FamilyLife Publishing
Dennis Rainey, President
5800 Ranch Drive
Little Rock, Arkansas 72223
(501) 223-8663 • www.familylife.com

11 10 09 08 07 06 05   1 2 3 4 5 6 7

ISBN: 1-57229-716-6

Author:	Bill and Carolyn Wellons
Editor:	Amy L. Bradford
Proofreader:	Fran Taylor
Graphic Designer:	Jerry McCall
Cover photo:	Getty Images (used by permission)

Table of Contents

Getting Away to Get It Together

Part One

Getting
Away

Why We Get Away

from Bill

Carolyn and I got married on December 20, 1970. We were in our early twenties when we exchanged vows, and I can assure you that we knew very little about developing and leading a lifelong partnership.

However, approximately ten years and two children later, we discovered something that has become the best single investment we have ever made in our marriage. It helps reconnect us when busyness robs us of emotional closeness. When the pace of life drains our strength and causes confusion, it re-energizes our partnership and helps clarify our vision as a couple. Our secret is simple: we schedule time to leave town—just the two of us—escaping from all the pressures at work, demands of people, and the responsibilities of home life. We call it *getting away to get it together!*

These retreats are diverse. We may relax at a friend's lake house, camp at a state park, or book a resort condominium in the off-season. But wherever we stay, God has continued to teach us to step off life's treadmill and examine the health of our relationship. When we evaluate where we are heading, we reap a fabulous return on investment.

Sure, there have been seasons when we missed "getting out of Dodge," but overall, our bi-annual retreats for two nights or more have consistently re-energized and enriched our togetherness.

Getting Away to Get It Together

Of course, the idea of retreating to put things into perspective is not original to us. In fact, Jesus was the master of getting away to get it together. I find several examples in the Bible of the Savior escaping the demands of the multitudes in favor of resting and refocusing alone. I share this because He is a wonderful model to imitate if you want your times away to be meaningful and worthwhile. Carolyn and I have included a few personal examples of our attempts at following in our Savior's footsteps (see The Master at Getting Away, page 4). It is our prayer that you enjoy your getaway experiences as much as we have. May God richly bless your relationship as you honor Him by making your marriage a priority.

Why We Getaway

Extra Copies

Before you begin your getaway, thumb through the checklists and Toolbox Projects and determine if you would like to make extra copies of these pages. This guide is intended to be reused, so some duplicates are provided; however, you may wish to use a photocopy or remove a page from the manual for writing comfort. Feel free to photocopy the checklists and worksheets for your own private use.

The Master at Getting Away

from Carolyn

Jesus was the master at getting away to put things into perspective. Even at the pinnacle of miraculous ministry with the multitudes, He would call for a time-out in favor of refocusing with His Father alone. If you want your times away to be meaningful and worthwhile, follow His examples of getting away to get it together.

First, I see Him getting away for times of personal prayer. After feeding the multitudes with five fish and two loaves of bread—no small undertaking—Matthew reports that "after He had sent the crowds away, He went up on the mountain by Himself to pray; and when it was evening, He was there alone" (Matthew 14:23, NASB).

Dr. Luke adds that during a time when "large crowds were gathering to hear Him and to be healed of their sicknesses ... Jesus Himself would often slip away to the wilderness and pray" (Luke 5:15-16).

One of my biggest getaway needs is for time all alone with the Lord. In fact, it is my first priority.

After a relaxing dinner together and a good night's sleep, I meet privately with the Lord. I take my Bible and journal in search of a quiet place for a personal quiet time.

It is important for me to feel in touch with my heavenly Father and to be in a right frame of mind before meeting with Bill later in the day. I begin with praise and adoration for who God is. Then, in a time of confession, I ask Him to reveal my sin to me. As I wait quietly, He reminds me of areas that need my repentance. I name these to Him and ask for forgiveness. This cleansing process ushers in a period of grateful thanksgiving for God's grace and mercy.

Then, I ask the Lord to reveal Himself to me in His Word. I read a chapter from the Bible, making notes of the highlights He shows me. As the passage dictates, I either pray the verses back to God for my life or identify a specific application in my life for that day.

Having pursued the mind of Christ, I feel spiritually refreshed and ready to join Bill for our lunchtime conversations.

> *Clearly, one activity that will make your getaway meaningful is making time to discuss personal issues with your heavenly Father.*

from Bill

Second, the Scriptures teach us that Jesus got away to make major decisions. A case in point was His choosing of the twelve disciples. The Bible says, "It was at this time that He went off to the mountain to pray, and He spent the whole night in prayer to God. And when day came, He called His disciples to Him and chose twelve of them, whom He also named as apostles" (Luke 6:12-13).

A perfect opportunity for a getaway retreat arose one summer when I was invited to do some consulting in South Carolina. Following my work, Carolyn and I spent several days just across the border in the small community of Brevard, North Carolina, with its spectacular views of the Smoky Mountains. We did our share of sight-seeing and spent time walking in a secluded area to talk and pray together each morning.

It was during this getaway that the Lord gave us unity about selling our home of twenty-four years and downsizing for our future. Carolyn and I had prayed about this matter and discussed it for years without resolving the issue. Because we did not agree on the timing, we decided upon waiting to make a move. While I had been ready to move earlier, Carolyn understandably wanted to raise all our children through their high school years in our family home. It was filled with memories and located very conveniently to our friends, our church, and our children's school.

Now at this point, our children were grown. Two were married with children of their own and a third was living on his own while working full-time and finishing college. It was as if God knew we were truly ready to move and dream about fresh possibilities for a new living situation in our new season of life.

During this getaway, we agreed to trust God to sell our home, which He did upon our return to Little Rock. We then took the next bold step and moved into an apartment (our "second honeymoon" love nest!) while shopping for the best location and layout of our new home. A major decision was finalized, and we were excited about our direction.

Your getaway is a perfect time to create an uninterrupted setting for working through a major decision you are facing as a couple.

from Carolyn

Third, the Savior got away to intercede for the benefit of others. Just before Jesus tells Peter that he will deny Him three times, we are told that the Lord said to him, "Simon, Simon, behold, Satan has demanded permission to sift you like wheat; but I have prayed for you, that your faith may not fail; and you, when once you have turned again, strengthen your brothers" (Luke 22:31-32).

While I enjoy resting, relaxing, and connecting with Bill emotionally, my favorite reason to get away is to pray for those I love. I cherish how this time allows me to bring the needs of family and friends before the Lord without interruption. Too often the pace of my daily life limits this practice. So I relish the satisfaction that comes from an undistracted, extended time with my heavenly Father.

I enjoy getting on my knees when I seek God's face on behalf of loved ones. This posture reminds me of who is in control of all the issues I present. Often, I pray verses of Scripture for those for whom I am interceding. I especially like the apostle Paul's prayers from Ephesians 1:17-19, Philippians 1:9-11, and Colossians 1:9-11. Still other times, I sit quietly allowing the Holy Spirit to guide my prayers for others.

There are several good prayer helps that I have discovered over the years. Two include Praying God's Will *by Beth Moore and* The Power of Praying for Your Husband *by Stormie Omartian. (The same author has also written about praying for your wife and children.)*

I also keep a journal of my intercessory prayer requests to review on future getaways. I've found that God does not answer every prayer immediately, and I continue to intercede for those requests. But as I read my journal, I recognize the many prayers that have been answered. I share these with Bill and we rejoice in God's love and provision.

Interceding for the needs of family, friends, church leaders, the sick and hurting, missionaries, government leaders, etc., makes for time well spent on your getaway.

from Bill

Finally, the Bible reveals that Jesus got away to address an unwanted circumstance in His life. Our Savior's experience in the Garden of Gethsemane illustrates this vividly:

> *They came to a place named Gethsemane; and He said to His disciples, "Sit here until I have prayed." And He took with Him Peter and James and John, and began to be very distressed and troubled. And He said to them, "My soul is deeply grieved to the point of death; remain here and keep watch." And He went a little beyond them, and fell to the ground and began to pray that if it were possible, the hour might pass Him by. And He was saying, "Abba! Father! All things are possible for You; remove this cup from Me; yet not what I will, but what You will." And He came and found them sleeping, and said to Peter, "Simon, are you asleep? Could you not keep watch for one hour? Keep watching and praying that you may not come into temptation; the spirit is willing, but the flesh is weak." Again He went away and prayed, saying the same words. And again He came and found them sleeping, for their eyes were very heavy; and they did not know what to answer Him. And He came the third time, and said to them, "Are you still sleeping and resting? It is enough; the hour has come; behold, the Son of Man is being betrayed into the hands of sinners. Get up, let us be going; behold, the one who betrays Me is at hand!*
>
> —Mark 14:32-42

Over the years, Carolyn and I have faced a number of unwanted circumstances in our marriage. These include the premature loss of our fathers and my mother, conflict between us or with a close friend, financial pressure, vocational frustration, a miscarriage, child-raising difficulties, kidney stones, etc.

However, the unwanted circumstance that shook us the most was when Carolyn's doctor told us she had cancer. I have never been more surprised and unprepared in my entire life. Fear of the future took hold, with overwhelming "what if" and "why" questions flooding our minds. It felt as though everything else in our lives stopped, and all of our time and attention focused on this disease.

Surgery followed by chemotherapy and various challenging side effects made life unpleasant, uncomfortable, and even lonely at times. We asked God, "Why us?" We wanted Him to "remove this cup" from us. We were distressed and troubled. For months we addressed this difficult situation on a daily basis, having no control over the disease. We were utterly dependent on God's healing power over our enemy.

Over time and by God's grace, our attitudes began to shift from "not what I will" to "Thy will be done." And that is when freedom arrived. Our peace began to grow because our perspective began to change.

God is greater than any unwanted circumstance. He is our only hope, our refuge, and our strength. And He continues to help us address our unwanted circumstances today.

God taught us much about life during this difficult season. Following chemotherapy, we celebrated together on an unforgettable getaway retreat in Maui. And I am pleased to report that Carolyn is free from cancer.

Your getaway provides a perfect opportunity for addressing a difficult situation in your life.

Frequently Asked Questions

Through the years, we have been asked repeatedly, "What do you do on your getaways?" The following questions and answers will reveal some of the practical lessons we have learned that make for a meaningful getaway experience. Be sure to read these before your getaway.

Carolyn and I have included a number of the projects in the Getaway Toolbox that we have developed and still use when we escape together. We have also added several stories from our personal experiences, so watch for them. Our prayer is that they will stimulate some helpful conversations.

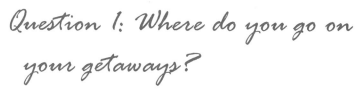

Question 1: Where do you go on your getaways?

Sometimes in the fall, we have enjoyed relaxing in a pop-up camper or cabin in one of Arkansas' state parks. For a winter getaway, we have taken advantage of off-season rates at a nearby resort or hotel. On other occasions, friends have made their lake house or condominium available to us. While the location is important, getting out of town is most critical.

Question 2: How many days do you recommend?

Plan on at least two nights away. While we have taken some one-night retreats, we've found time and again that a minimum of two nights away provides the time we need to unwind, to have meaningful conversations, and to avoid feeling rushed to get back home.

Question 3: What preparations do we need to make?

The first things that come to mind are budget, schedule, and travel plans. While these are important, consider these other critical details: tending to your children's needs (especially young children), discussing each other's expectations and adjusting your own, and praying in advance for God to lead you.

Children—Men, imagine how distracted you wife will be if she's not secure about your children's well-being. While you're away, provide the best solution possible. This may include finding a sitter or family with whom your children (and you) are comfortable, joining a baby-sitting co-op, or swapping weekends with the parents of your children's friends—your kids stay the weekend there, and in return, you keep their children for a weekend later on.

Expectations—A friend once told me, "All conflict is the result of differing assumptions or expectations." With that in mind, take the initiative to discuss each other's expectations a few days before you leave. (See Getaway Expectations on page 18.) How does each of you envision spending your time away? Reading a good book? Some alone time? Resting? Taking walks together? A fun activity? Is there a pressing issue that needs your focused attention? Which projects in the Getaway Toolbox would be most helpful?

Work through your Getaway Expectations before you leave home. As you do so, keep in mind that every agenda item does not need to be nailed down. In

Getting Away to Get It Together

fact, leave some room for spontaneity and fun. Once you're sure you understand each other's hopes and needs, agree generally on the overall plan for your getaway.

Prayer—Finally, pray in advance, asking the Lord to prepare your hearts and guide your discussions. Invite His presence and power to enrich your relationship and make your time together significant.

Special Note: Toolbox project 3: Memorial Stones and Toolbox Project 4: Calendar Coordination are two of our favorites! You will need your personal calendars and pens or pencils for these. Toolbox Project 6: Your Unique Design© also requires some advance work. See page 73 for more details.

Question 4: What does a typical schedule look like?

Breaking away from the office, arranging childcare, and packing will take its toll. On occasion, you'll look at each other as you leave town and ask, as we have, "Is it really worth it?" Well, it really is. The following suggested schedule assumes you leave home mid-afternoon the first day and return home mid-afternoon on the third day. It is described in three one-day snapshots to help you get a feel for planning your own getaway experience.

Scheduling

First Day Snapshot

Travel to your getaway location, get settled, and spend a quiet dinner alone. You can select any project that you like for discussion at dinner. We have found taking turns answering a few of the Why Questions in Toolbox Project 1 (page 42) to be simple and fun, providing for some stimulating conversation. Connecting is the name of the game—the more conversation, the better. So just relax and enjoy being together.

Second Day Snapshot

Determine your own schedule for meals, personal relaxation, romance, and fun. You can select one or more projects in the Getaway Toolbox for this day, perhaps one for the morning and one for the afternoon. Carolyn and I have found the Memorial Stones in Toolbox Project 3 (page 48) is a wonderful way to begin this day. Set aside some time in the afternoon to interact over a pressing issue that you identified when discussing your getaway expectations, or select a second project from the Toolbox. Spend the remainder of the day as you please.

Third Day Snapshot

As with the second day, there is plenty of flexibility for you to set your own pace. The goal is not to complete every project in the toolbox; it is to enjoy the process of meaningful, uninterrupted communication. However, before you leave for home, we highly recommend completing the Calendar Coordination in Toolbox Project 4 (page 59). This requires your personal calendars and any other school, business, or church information pertinent to your schedules. While doing this, be sure to set the date for your next getaway, ideally in six months. We hope this is helpful.

Now, customize a plan for your getaway and have a great time!

Question 5: What have you learned from getting away together?

Most importantly, we've learned that the spiritual warfare described in Ephesians 6:10-12 threatens our marriage constantly, and we need a counterattack. As we've invested in getaways twice yearly, we've found that we're more emotionally connected and spiritually proactive. This helps us defeat the challenges of the enemy.

Summary

Why getaway?

Jesus models "getting away to get it together" by using His time apart for:

1. Personal prayer
2. Decision making
3. Intercessory prayer
4. Unwanted circumstances

We've found that getting away is a proactive investment in our marriage that helps us connect emotionally and defeat the challenges of the enemy.

How do we plan a getaway?

1. Pray about your getaway concerns and ask for God's help: money, time, location, childcare, etc.
2. Evaluate your schedules and choose a date.
3. Estimate expenses and funds available.
4. Decide on location, make lodging and travel reservations.
5. Arrange childcare.
6. Discuss expectations, complete Toolbox Project 1.
7. Pray for God's leadership and your willingness to follow.

Where?

Get out of town.
To save money:

- Camp
- Borrow a lakehouse
- Book a location during the off-season

How long?

Two nights minimum

Suggested Schedule

Day One: Arrive, unpack, enjoy your dinner discussion and toolbox project of your choice (Project 1 is suggested).

Day Two: Take your time for meals, relaxation, romance, fun, and choose one or two projects from the toolbox—you determine the order of events.

Day Three: Select another toolbox project (Project 4 is good), schedule your next getaway.

Getaway Expectations

Prior to getting away, we briefly discuss our expectations about how our time will be invested. We also identify a few of the projects in the Getaway Toolbox that we want to cover on our retreat.

Though the following exercise certainly isn't *required* for you to have a great getaway experience, it *may* help you agree on your overall expectations and, therefore, avoid conflict or disappointment once you arrive. Consider working through this exercise a few days before you leave.

STEP 1: Using scratch paper, separately write out your expectations for your getaway.

STEP 2: Still working separately, skim the Toolbox Projects in pages 42-95, and on your scratch paper, jot down a couple that seem most beneficial to you.

STEP 3: Come together and share your expectations and explain why you feel your selected projects would be helpful.

STEP 4: Come to an agreement on your mutual expectations and write them on the lines labeled "Our Getaway Expectations" on the "Getaway 1" section on page 20. Be sure they are reasonable, especially if this is your first getaway.

STEP 5: Determine which toolbox projects you would like to complete as a couple and check them below. Use the "If you need … " suggestions on the following page to guide you in finding projects that fit.

Getaway Verse

And let us consider how to stimulate one another to love and good deeds.
—Hebrews 10:24

If you need ...

Rest, relaxation, and restoration, then try

❑ Why Questions: a simple way to learn something new about each other (Toolbox Project 1)

❑ Memorial Stones: mark life's progress; celebrate God's goodness (Toolbox Project 3)

Connection and intimacy, then try

❑ Why Questions: a simple way to learn something new about each other (Toolbox Project 1)

❑ Memorial Stones: mark life's progress; celebrate God's goodness (Toolbox Project 3)

❑ Calendar Coordination: stake out time for what's really important (Toolbox Project 4)

❑ Child Talk: intentionality in training your young ones (Toolbox Project 7)

❑ Leaving a Legacy: putting your family values on paper (Toolbox Project 8)

Organization and direction, then try

❑ Single-Word Descriptions: target an area of life you'd like to improve (Toolbox Project 2)

❑ Calendar Coordination: stake out time for what's really important (Toolbox Project 4)

❑ My Bagel: finding life's center and re-balancing it all (Toolbox Project 5)

❑ Your Unique Design©: discovering and living in your giftedness (Toolbox Project 6)

❑ Child Talk: intentionality in training your young ones (Toolbox Project 7)

❑ Leaving a Legacy: putting your family values on paper (Toolbox Project 8)

❑ Financially Faithful: investing in blessing (Toolbox Project 9)

❑ Most-Wanted List: bringing others along in your walk with God (Toolbox Project 10)

Fun and adventure, then try

❑ Why Questions: a simple way to learn something new about each other (Toolbox Project 1)

❑ Memorial Stones: mark life's progress; celebrate God's goodness (Toolbox Project 3)

❑ Your Unique Design: discovering and living in your giftedness (Toolbox Project 6)

❑ Financially Faithful: investing in blessing (Toolbox Project 9)

❑ Most-Wanted List: bringing others along in your walk with God (Toolbox Project 10)

Getaway Expectations 1

Our Getaway Expectations

_____

_____

_____

_____

Our Toolbox Projects

❑ Project 1—Why Questions: a simple way to learn something new about each other

❑ Project 2—Single-Word Descriptions: target an area of life you'd like to improve

❑ Project 3—Memorial Stones: mark life's progress; celebrate God's goodness

❑ Project 4—Calendar Coordination: stake out time for what's really important

❑ Project 5—My Bagel: finding life's center and re-balancing it all

❑ Project 6—Your Unique Design©: discovering and living in your giftedness

❑ Project 7—Child Talk: intentionality in training your young ones

❑ Project 8—Leaving a Legacy: putting your family values on paper

❑ Project 9—Financially Faithful: investing in blessing

❑ Project 10—Most-Wanted List: bringing others along in your walk with God

Getaway Expectations 2

Our Getaway Expectations

_____

_____

_____

_____

_____

Our Toolbox Projects

- ❑ Project 1—Why Questions: a simple way to learn something new about each other

- ❑ Project 2—Single-Word Descriptions: target an area of life you'd like to improve

- ❑ Project 3—Memorial Stones: mark life's progress; celebrate God's goodness

- ❑ Project 4—Calendar Coordination: stake out time for what's really important

- ❑ Project 5—My Bagel: finding life's center and re-balancing it all

- ❑ Project 6—Your Unique Design©: discovering and living in your giftedness

- ❑ Project 7—Child Talk: intentionality in training your young ones

- ❑ Project 8—Leaving a Legacy: putting your family values on paper

- ❑ Project 9—Financially Faithful: investing in blessing

- ❑ Project 10—Most-Wanted List: bringing others along in your walk with God

Getaway Expectations 3

Our Getaway Expectations

_____

_____

_____

_____

Our Toolbox Projects

❑ Project 1—Why Questions: a simple way to learn something new about each other

❑ Project 2—Single-Word Descriptions: target an area of life you'd like to improve

❑ Project 3—Memorial Stones: mark life's progress; celebrate God's goodness

❑ Project 4—Calendar Coordination: stake out time for what's really important

❑ Project 5—My Bagel: finding life's center and re-balancing it all

❑ Project 6—Your Unique Design©: discovering and living in your giftedness

❑ Project 7—Child Talk: intentionality in training your young ones

❑ Project 8—Leaving a Legacy: putting your family values on paper

❑ Project 9—Financially Faithful: investing in blessing

❑ Project 10—Most-Wanted List: bringing others along in your walk with God

Getaway Expectations 4

Our Getaway Expectations

_____

_____

_____

_____

_____

Our Toolbox Projects

❑ Project 1—Why Questions: a simple way to learn something new about each other

❑ Project 2—Single-Word Descriptions: target an area of life you'd like to improve

❑ Project 3—Memorial Stones: mark life's progress; celebrate God's goodness

❑ Project 4—Calendar Coordination: stake out time for what's really important

❑ Project 5—My Bagel: finding life's center and re-balancing it all

❑ Project 6—Your Unique Design©: discovering and living in your giftedness

❑ Project 7—Child Talk: intentionality in training your young ones

❑ Project 8—Leaving a Legacy: putting your family values on paper

❑ Project 9—Financially Faithful: investing in blessing

❑ Project 10—Most-Wanted List: bringing others along in your walk with God

Getaway Preparations

Throughout the book, we've suggested making certain preparations and bringing certain items to get the most from your getaway. These are included here along with a few other reminders that will help make your getaway planning simple. Copy this sheet and keep it with you as you plan, or tear out one of the multiple copies from this book.

Important Information - Getaway 1

Location _____

Hotel name _____

City, State _____ Phone _____

Dates _____ Our cell phone _____

Child- or pet-care provider _____

Address_____ Home phone _____

Cell phone _____ Other contact number_____

Neighbor or other emergency contact _____

Relation: neighbor, family, etc. _____

Address _____

Phone _____ Cell phone _____

Tip: Photocopy the Important Information section for your care provider. It's a simple way to exchange the necessary contact and emergency phone numbers.

Preparation Checklist - Getaway 1

A Month or Two Before

- ❑ start praying for your getaway
- ❑ reserve lodging
- ❑ schedule childcare and/or pet care
- ❑ book rental car or flights if needed

_____

_____

_____

Four or Five Days Before

- ❑ continue praying
- ❑ get seven-day weather forecast (weather.com)
- ❑ get directions to your destination (atlas, map, mapquest.com)
- ❑ confirm childcare and/or pet care
- ❑ wash laundry and iron
- ❑ drop off/pick up dry cleaning
- ❑ for Toolbox Project 6: Complete the Servants by Design™ Inventory at www.youruniquedesign.com. Your profile will arrive within twenty-four hours via e-mail.

_____

_____

_____

Getting Away to Get It Together

A Day or Two Before

❑ pray
❑ pack according to weather forecast
❑ water houseplants
❑ ask neighbor to pick up mail or newspapers
❑ charge camera batteries, cell phones

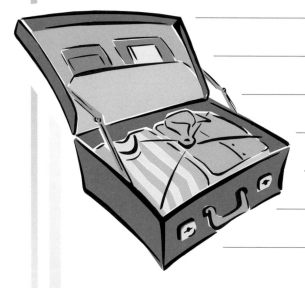

_____

_____

_____

_____

_____

Day of

❑ keep praying!
❑ if needed, confirm flights
❑ pack last-minute items (toothbrush, toiletries)
❑ deliver children/pets to caretakers

_____

_____

_____

_____

Packing Checklist - Getaway 1

- ❑ directions to destination, map
- ❑ cell phone, charger, adapter
- ❑ Bible
- ❑ book or magazine
- ❑ journal or blank paper
- ❑ pens, pencils, highlighters
- ❑ this book and this list
- ❑ for Your Unique Design©: your Servants by Design™ Inventory
- ❑ for Calendar Coordination: a blank calendar for a combined family calendar and his and her calendars, day planners, or PDAs
- ❑ snacks
- ❑ toiletries
- ❑ hair dryer
- ❑ medicines, vitamins
- ❑ sunscreen
- ❑ clothing
  - • shirts
  - • shoes, sandals, or boots
  - • outerwear
  - • pants/skirts
  - • socks
  - • swimwear
  - • underclothes
  - • belt
  - • hat

Notes:

_____

_____

_____

_____

_____

Important Information - Getaway 2

Location _____

Hotel name _____

City, State _____ Phone_____

Dates _____ Our cell phone _____

Child- or pet-care provider _____

Address_____ Home phone _____

Cell phone _____ Other contact number_____

Neighbor or other emergency contact _____

Relation: neighbor, family, etc. _____

Address_____

Phone _____ Cell phone _____

_____

_____

_____

_____

Tip: Photocopy the Important Information section for your care provider. It's a simple way to exchange the necessary contact and emergency phone numbers.

Preparation Checklist - Getaway 2

A Month or Two Before

- ❑ start praying for your getaway
- ❑ reserve lodging
- ❑ schedule childcare and/or pet care
- ❑ book rental car or flights if needed

_____

_____

_____

_____

Four or Five Days Before

- ❑ continue praying
- ❑ get seven-day weather forecast (weather.com)
- ❑ get directions to your destination (atlas, map, mapquest.com)
- ❑ confirm childcare and/or pet care
- ❑ wash laundry and iron
- ❑ drop off/pick up dry cleaning
- ❑ for Toolbox Project 6: Complete the Servants by Design™ Inventory at www.youruniquedesign.com. Your profile will arrive within twenty-four hours via e-mail.

_____

_____

_____

_____

A Day or Two Before

- ❑ pray
- ❑ pack according to weather forecast
- ❑ water houseplants
- ❑ ask neighbor to pick up mail or newspapers
- ❑ charge camera batteries, cell phones

_____

_____

_____

_____

_____

Day of

- ❑ keep praying!
- ❑ if needed, confirm flights
- ❑ pack last-minute items (toothbrush, toiletries)
- ❑ deliver children/pets to caretakers

_____

_____

_____

Packing Checklist - Getaway 2

- ❑ directions to destination, map
- ❑ cell phone, charger, adapter
- ❑ Bible
- ❑ book or magazine
- ❑ journal or blank paper
- ❑ pens, pencils, highlighters
- ❑ this book and this list
- ❑ for Your Unique Design©: your Servants by Design™ Inventory
- ❑ for Calendar Coordination: a blank calendar for a combined family calendar and his and her calendars, day planners, or PDAs
- ❑ snacks
- ❑ toiletries
- ❑ hair dryer
- ❑ medicines, vitamins
- ❑ sunscreen
- ❑ clothing
  - shirts
  - shoes, sandals, or boots
  - outerwear
  - pants/skirts
  - socks
  - swimwear
  - underclothes
  - belt
  - hat

Notes:

_____

_____

_____

_____

_____

_____

Important Information - Getaway 3

Location _____

Hotel name _____

City, State _____ Phone _____

Dates _____ Our cell phone _____

Child- or pet-care provider _____

Address _____ Home phone _____

Cell phone _____ Other contact number _____

Neighbor or other emergency contact _____

Relation: neighbor, family, etc. _____

Address _____

Phone _____ Cell phone _____

_____

_____

_____

_____

Tip: Photocopy the Important Information section for your care provider. It's a simple way to exchange the necessary contact and emergency phone numbers.

Preparation Checklist - Getaway 3

A Month or Two Before

- ❑ start praying for your getaway
- ❑ reserve lodging
- ❑ schedule childcare and/or pet care
- ❑ book rental car or flights if needed

_____

_____

_____

_____

Four or Five Days Before

- ❑ continue praying
- ❑ get seven-day weather forecast (weather.com)
- ❑ get directions to your destination (atlas, map, mapquest.com)
- ❑ confirm childcare and/or pet care
- ❑ wash laundry and iron
- ❑ drop off/pick up dry cleaning
- ❑ for Toolbox Project 6: Complete the Servants by Design™ Inventory at www.youruniquedesign.com. Your profile will arrive within twenty-four hours via e-mail.

_____

_____

_____

_____

A Day or Two Before

- ❑ pray
- ❑ pack according to weather forecast
- ❑ water houseplants
- ❑ ask neighbor to pick up mail or newspapers
- ❑ charge camera batteries, cell phones

_____

_____

_____

_____

_____

Day of

- ❑ keep praying!
- ❑ if needed, confirm flights
- ❑ pack last-minute items (toothbrush, toiletries)
- ❑ deliver children/pets to caretakers

_____

_____

_____

_____

Packing Checklist - Getaway 3

- ❑ directions to destination, map
- ❑ cell phone, charger, adapter
- ❑ Bible
- ❑ book or magazine
- ❑ journal or blank paper
- ❑ pens, pencils, highlighters
- ❑ this book and this list
- ❑ for Your Unique Design©: your Servants by Design™ Inventory
- ❑ for Calendar Coordination: a blank calendar for a combined family calendar and his and her calendars, day planners, or PDAs
- ❑ snacks
- ❑ toiletries
- ❑ hair dryer
- ❑ medicines, vitamins
- ❑ sunscreen
- ❑ clothing
  - shirts
  - shoes, sandals, or boots
  - outerwear
  - pants/skirts
  - socks
  - swimwear
  - underclothes
  - belt
  - hat

Notes:

_____

_____

_____

_____

_____

_____

Important Information - Getaway 4

Location _____

Hotel name _____

City, State _____ Phone _____

Dates _____ Our cell phone _____

Child- or pet-care provider _____

Address _____ Home phone _____

Cell phone _____ Other contact number _____

Neighbor or other emergency contact _____

Relation: neighbor, family, etc. _____

Address _____

Phone _____ Cell phone _____

_____

_____

_____

_____

Tip: Photocopy the Important Information section for your care provider. It's a simple way to exchange the necessary contact and emergency phone numbers.

Preparation Checklist - Getaway 4

A Month or Two Before

- ☐ start praying for your getaway
- ☐ reserve lodging
- ☐ schedule childcare and/or pet care
- ☐ book rental car or flights if needed

_____

_____

_____

_____

Four or Five Days Before

- ☐ continue praying
- ☐ get seven-day weather forecast (weather.com)
- ☐ get directions to your destination (atlas, map, mapquest.com)
- ☐ confirm childcare and/or pet care
- ☐ wash laundry and iron
- ☐ drop off/pick up dry cleaning
- ☐ for Toolbox Project 6: Complete the Servants by Design™ Inventory at www.youruniquedesign.com. Your profile will arrive within twenty-four hours via e-mail.

_____

_____

_____

_____

A Day or Two Before

- ☐ pray
- ☐ pack according to weather forecast
- ☐ water houseplants
- ☐ ask neighbor to pick up mail or newspapers
- ☐ charge camera batteries, cell phones

_____

_____

_____

_____

_____

_____

Day of

- ☐ keep praying!
- ☐ if needed, confirm flights
- ☐ pack last-minute items (toothbrush, toiletries)
- ☐ deliver children/pets to caretakers

_____

_____

_____

Packing Checklist - Getaway 4

❑ directions to destination, map
❑ cell phone, charger, adapter
❑ Bible
❑ book or magazine
❑ journal or blank paper
❑ pens, pencils, highlighters
❑ this book and this list
❑ for Your Unique Design©: your Servants by Design™ Inventory
❑ for Calendar Coordination: a blank calendar for a combined family calendar and his and her calendars, day planners, or PDAs
❑ snacks
❑ toiletries
❑ hair dryer
❑ medicines, vitamins
❑ sunscreen
❑ clothing

- shirts
- shoes, sandals, or boots
- outerwear
- pants/skirts
- socks
- swimwear
- underclothes
- belt
- hat

Notes:

_____

_____

_____

_____

_____

_____

Getting Away _to Get It_ Together

Part Two

Getaway Toolbox

Why Questions

A simple way to learn something new about each other

Take a few moments to read all of the Why Questions. As you do, identify those you would like your spouse to answer. Then take turns answering these questions. You may answer several questions or just a few. The point is to enjoy having time to relate without interruptions.

❦ If you had $10,000,000 cash, tax free, how would you spend the rest of your life?

❦ Describe your dream vacation. Where would you go, who would go with you, and what would you want to do? Explain why this would be fun for you.

❦ Name a person (other than your spouse) who has made a significant contribution to your life. Tell how you were influenced by this individual.

❦ Galatians 5:22-23 lists the fruits of the Spirit: "love, joy, peace, patience, kindness, goodness, faithfulness, gentleness, [and] self control." Select which of these you most want to develop and tell why.

❦ Tell your spouse one aspect of his/her personality that you appreciate. Describe the impact of this character trait in your life and the lives of others.

❦ Share with your spouse the things that energize you at work, in ministry, or in your personal hobbies.

- Describe yourself as a color. Tell why you chose that particular color.

- Share one dream you have for the future and explain its importance to you.

- What passage of Scripture do you find meaningful for your marriage and why?

- What has God been teaching you about yourself? Reveal how He has done this and the value you are gaining from it.

- Share one of the most meaningful gifts you have ever received. Why was this one so significant?

- Identify an area of your life in which you want to grow over the next year and explain why.

His Single-Word Descriptions

Target an area of life you'd like to improve

Separately, take a few minutes to record a single-word description of where you are emotionally in the following seven areas of your life. Be creative and honest, and be prepared to explain the reason for your answers. When you and your wife are finished, take turns sharing your descriptive words. Write down each other's responses in the last column. His and her pages have been provided.

Area of Life	My Single Word	My Wife's Single Word
Physical		
Spiritual		
Relational (friends)		
Vocational		
Marital		
Financial		
Familial (children, grandchildren)		

When you are through sharing, circle one area you would like to improve this year. What action steps will you take? Record your ideas here:

_____

_____

_____

Conclude your time together in prayer, asking for God's power and direction to succeed.

Her Single-Word Descriptions

Target an area of life you'd like to improve

Date completed:

_____

Area of Life	My Single Word	My Husband's Single Word
Physical		
Spiritual		
Relational (friends)		
Vocational		
Marital		
Financial		
Familial (children, grandchildren)		

When you are through sharing, circle one area you would like to improve this year. What action steps will you take? Record your ideas here:

_____

_____

_____

Conclude your time together in prayer, asking for God's power and direction to succeed.

Getaway Verses

Trust in the Lord with all your heart and do not lean on your own understanding. In all your ways acknowledge Him, and He will make your paths straight. Do not be wise in your own eyes; fear the Lord and turn away from evil.

—Proverbs 3:5-7

His Single-Word Descriptions

Target an area of life you'd like to improve

Date completed:

_____

Area of Life	My Single Word	My Wife's Single Word
Physical		
Spiritual		
Relational (friends)		
Vocational		
Marital		
Financial		
Familial (children, grandchildren)		

When you are through sharing, circle one area you would like to improve this year. What action steps will you take? Record your ideas here:

_____

_____

_____

Conclude your time together in prayer, asking for God's power and direction to succeed.

Getaway Verses

Trust in the Lord with all your heart and do not lean on your own understanding. In all your ways acknowledge Him, and He will make your paths straight. Do not be wise in your own eyes; fear the Lord and turn away from evil.

—Proverbs 3:5-7

Her Single-Word Descriptions

Target an area of life you'd like to improve

Area of Life	My Single Word	My Husband's Single Word
Physical		
Spiritual		
Relational (friends)		
Vocational		
Marital		
Financial		
Familial (children, grandchildren)		

When you are through sharing, circle one area you would like to improve this year. What action steps will you take? Record your ideas here:

_____

_____

_____

Conclude your time together in prayer, asking for God's power and direction to succeed.

Getaway Verses

Trust in the Lord with all your heart and do not lean on your own understanding. In all your ways acknowledge Him, and He will make your paths straight. Do not be wise in your own eyes; fear the Lord and turn away from evil.

—Proverbs 3:5-7

Memorial Stones

Mark life's progress; celebrate God's goodness

from Bill

In the Old Testament book of Joshua, we find the Lord, through His servant Joshua, encouraging the Israelites to erect a memorial of twelve stones.

> *Now the people came up from the Jordan on the tenth of the first month and camped at Gilgal on the eastern edge of Jericho. Those twelve stones which they had taken from the Jordan, Joshua set up at Gilgal. He said to the sons of Israel, "When your children ask their fathers in time to come, saying, 'What are these stones?' then you shall inform your children, saying, 'Israel crossed this Jordan on dry ground.' For the Lord your God dried up the waters of the Jordan before you until you had crossed, just as the Lord your God had done to the Red Sea, which He dried up before us until we had crossed; that all the peoples of the earth may know that the hand of the Lord is mighty, so that you may fear the Lord your God forever."*
>
> —Joshua 4:19-24

Notice that the purpose of these memorial stones was to encourage confidence in God for things present and future.

> *Carolyn and I particularly enjoy and benefit from this project. It helps us identify and celebrate the faithfulness and grace of God in our lives. Oftentimes we will start by remembering some of the spiritual memorial stones that He has so freely given to us. There are many wonderful passages in the Bible for doing this. One of our favorites is Psalm 103. It is packed with provisions of God's mercy that are worth remembering: He pardons, He heals, He redeems, He crowns, He*

satisfies. He has not dealt with us according to our sins. He is compassionate, forgiving, etc.

On many occasions, I am overwhelmed by God's love for me by simply reading this psalm and reflecting on His wonderful gifts in my life. This usually leads me to a time of praise and thanksgiving.

Then, using my calendar, journal, and even my job description for the year, I begin recalling the things God has allowed me to do over a six- to twelve-month period. I remember a year when I wrote about leading a neighbor to Jesus Christ. Seeing God transform my friend's life and grow him blessed me repeatedly. It made me feel like God was using me for something of eternal significance.

On another occasion, Carolyn and I had been invited to join the speaker team of FamilyLife, a marriage and family ministry of Campus Crusade for Christ. We were honored by the opportunity it gave us to minister together by sharing God's plan for marriage with others. What we saw God do in the lives of people at these conferences was miraculous! At times we could not believe He had chosen us to partner with Him. It is a memory of His faithfulness that we cherish.

Discipling a child at home, teaching a class at church, completing a project at work, resolving a conflict, watching one of your children succeed, remembering a trip, forming a new friendship, celebrating a new birth, talking with a loved one ... when it comes to your personal memorial stones, there are endless possibilities.

Stack some stones on your getaway. Your confidence and your love for the Lord will grow every time you do.

The simple exercise on the following page will help you and your spouse to identify your memorial stones from the past six to twelve months. Each of you can fill out the blank his-and-her forms that follow. When you have each completed steps one through three, come together and share with each other your memorial stones and how they encourage your confidence in the Lord.

His Memorial Stones

Step 1: Write out a list of practical memorial stones from the last six to twelve months of your life. These may include completed projects, critical decisions, lessons learned, a unique experience, or goals achieved. They may relate to your vocation, marriage, ministry to others, friendships, or personal life. Use the space below to record your responses.

✿ _____

✿ _____

✿ _____

✿ _____

✿ _____

✿ _____

✿ _____

✿ _____

Memorial Stones
from the Past 6-12 Months

Step 2: Circle the two memorial stones from your list in Step 1 that are most meaningful to you.

Step 3: Ask yourself (1) Why were these so meaningful to me? (2) How did each make me feel? (3) How did they encourage my confidence in the Lord? Record your thoughts below for sharing with your wife.

_____

_____

_____

_____

_____

_____

_____

Step 4: Take turns sharing your memorial stones. Conclude with a time of prayer, giving thanks to God for His provisions.

Getaway Verses

Bless the Lord, O my soul, and all that is within me, bless His holy name. Bless the Lord, O my soul, and forget none of His benefits; who pardons all your iniquities, who heals all your diseases; who redeems your life from the pit, who crowns you with lovingkindness and compassion; who satisfies your years with good things, so that your youth is renewed like the eagle.

—Psalm 103:1-5

Her Memorial Stones

Step 1: Write out a list of practical memorial stones from the last six to twelve months of your life. These may include completed projects, critical decisions, lessons learned, a unique experience, or goals achieved. They may relate to your vocation, marriage, ministry to others, friendships, or personal life. Use the space below to record your responses.

Date completed:

_____

❁ _____

❁ _____

❁ _____

❁ _____

❁ _____

❁ _____

❁ _____

❁ _____

Memorial Stones from the Past 6-12 Months

Step 2: Circle the two memorial stones from your list in Step 1 that are most meaningful to you.

Step 3: Ask yourself (1) Why were these so meaningful to me? (2) How did each make me feel? (3) How did they encourage my confidence in the Lord? Record your thoughts below for sharing with your husband.

_____

_____

_____

_____

_____

_____

_____

_____

Step 4: Take turns sharing your memorial stones. Conclude with a time of prayer, giving thanks to God for His provisions.

Getaway Verses

Bless the Lord, O my soul, and all that is within me, bless His holy name. Bless the Lord, O my soul, and forget none of His benefits; who pardons all your iniquities, who heals all your diseases; who redeems your life from the pit, who crowns you with lovingkindness and compassion; who satisfies your years with good things, so that your youth is renewed like the eagle.

—Psalm 103:1-5

His Memorial Stones

Step 1: Write out a list of practical memorial stones from the last six to twelve months of your life. These may include completed projects, critical decisions, lessons learned, a unique experience, or goals achieved. They may relate to your vocation, marriage, ministry to others, friendships, or personal life. Use the space below to record your responses.

❀ _____

❀ _____

❀ _____

❀ _____

❀ _____

❀ _____

❀ _____

❀ _____

Memorial Stones from the Past 6-12 Months

Step 2: Circle the two memorial stones from your list in Step 1 that are most meaningful to you.

Step 3: Ask yourself (1) Why were these so meaningful to me? (2) How did each make me feel? (3) How did they encourage my confidence in the Lord? Record your thoughts below for sharing with your wife.

_____

_____

_____

_____

_____

_____

_____

_____

Step 4: Take turns sharing your memorial stones. Conclude with a time of prayer, giving thanks to God for His provisions.

Getaway Verses

Bless the Lord, O my soul, and all that is within me, bless His holy name. Bless the Lord, O my soul, and forget none of His benefits; who pardons all your iniquities, who heals all your diseases; who redeems your life from the pit, who crowns you with lovingkindness and compassion; who satisfies your years with good things, so that your youth is renewed like the eagle.

—Psalm 103:1-5

Her Memorial Stones

Step 1: Write out a list of practical memorial stones from the last six to twelve months of your life. These may include completed projects, critical decisions, lessons learned, a unique experience, or goals achieved. They may relate to your vocation, marriage, ministry to others, friendships, or personal life. Use the space below to record your responses.

Date completed:

_____

❀ _____

❀ _____

❀ _____

❀ _____

❀ _____

❀ _____

❀ _____

❀ _____

Memorial Stones
from the Past 6-12 Months

Step 2: Circle the two memorial stones from your list in Step 1 that are most meaningful to you.

Step 3: Ask yourself (1) Why were these so meaningful to me? (2) How did each make me feel? (3) How did they encourage my confidence in the Lord? Record your thoughts below for sharing with your husband.

_____

_____

_____

_____

_____

_____

_____

Step 4: Take turns sharing your memorial stones. Conclude with a time of prayer, giving thanks to God for His provisions.

Getaway Verses

Bless the Lord, O my soul, and all that is within me, bless His holy name. Bless the Lord, O my soul, and forget none of His benefits; who pardons all your iniquities, who heals all your diseases; who redeems your life from the pit, who crowns you with lovingkindness and compassion; who satisfies your years with good things, so that your youth is renewed like the eagle.

—Psalm 103:1-5

Calendar Coordination

Stake out time for what's really important

from Carolyn

Calendar coordination will help you determine a manageable pace for your marriage and family and it allows you to make the most of your time. It will keep you from forgetting important dates, help you anticipate future events together, encourage you to pray for each other especially during demanding time periods, and allow you to reserve time for your marriage and family relationships.

If I have learned anything, it is the value of communicating with Bill about the family calendar. This helps us be proactive in determining the pace of our household, scheduling time for special moments and memories, and for knowing where we are heading as a couple. Without some calendar coordination, fishing with Grandpa never happens. Taking the children to Washington, D.C., gets squeezed out. That mission trip remains a dream instead of a life-changing reality.

Before we leave home, Bill and I gather our personal calendars, church calendar, school calendar, and any sports team or extracurricular activity calendars we need to coordinate. As we spread out these calendars on our getaway, we discuss social obligations and fun activities, dream about possible future trips to far-off places, and pray for God's leading as we begin to chart our course for the next six months.

We find the month-at-a-glance-style calendar helps us record our information. Often, we start with the non-negotiables: special events, birthdays, weddings, as well as certain school activities, church meetings, and appointments. When our children were young, we also blocked off time for family night each week. Next, we discuss dates for inviting friends for dinner and write them on our calendar. And then, my favorite part, we line up weekend experiences for the upcoming months, make holiday plans, and schedule family vacations. These outings provide us with countless memories to enjoy.

As we return home, our coordinated calendar helps us monitor the pace of our lives. It guides us in saying no to some opportunities in order to say yes to the best ones. It helps us keep our family time a priority and generally protects us from over-commitment. This exercise unifies us, strengthens our family relationships, ensures fond memories, and provides a sense of purpose and clarity of direction like nothing else we've ever done.

Both husband and wife must have their personal calendar to complete this exercise. If you have school-aged children, you also need the dates of important school events and church activities that affect your overall pace of life.

Step 1: Begin by exchanging important dates and information from your personal calendars one month at a time. Then identify upcoming events, commitments, or activities that are not yet on your calendar. Discuss these and add them now. Following is a list of idea starters for events that may require some family coordination.

- ❧ Children's special events
- ❧ Family nights
- ❧ Personal schedules/appointments
- ❧ Holidays, wedding anniversary, birthdays

- ❧ Family vacation
- ❧ Date nights
- ❧ Entertaining friends
- ❧ Projects at home
- ❧ Church and school meetings
- ❧ Your next getaway

Working in one-month blocks, coordinate your calendars until you've completed plans for at least the next six months. (We've found it helpful to have a general overview of our combined schedules one year in advance.)

Step 2: Is the pace you are setting reasonable and healthy? Did you block some time for family nights? Is there margin in your schedule for rest and relaxation? What do you need to say no to for the good of your marriage and home life?

Step 3: Agree on your coordinated six-month schedule. Commit this to the Lord and ask Him to empower you and guide you every step of the way.

Getaway Recommendation: If your personal calendars are too small to record your combined information, then after your getaway, develop a six month, month-at-a-glance-style calendar representing the results of your calendar coordination. Agree to complete and review this combined calendar together within two weeks of your getaway to keep you on track.

Getaway Verses

Therefore be careful how you walk, not as unwise men but as wise, making the most of your time, because the days are evil.

—Ephesians 5:15-16

Bill's Bagel

Finding life's center and re-balancing it all

from Bill

Jesus spoke these words to His disciples: "Let your light shine before men in such a way that they may see your good works, and glorify your Father who is in heaven" (Matthew 5:16). The exhortation to us is simple. We reveal our inner lives to others on the outside through everything we do. The bagel exercise is a great way to evaluate how well we are doing.

This exercise has given me a much more holistic view of my life and the good works that God wants me to do for Him.

I like to think of it this way. The Lord is my chief executive officer. Everything in my bagel represents my real job, not just my vocational responsibilities at the office. Also, I am on a direct reporting basis to the King of the universe for every area of my bagel. Those are big thoughts that bring a new perspective!

Notice a few of the insights the Lord revealed to me as I worked through my present bagel (current life-focus) and my future bagel (adjusted life-focus).

*My
Present
Bagel*

Hobbies

Friends

Boards

Family
Son (college)
Adult married
children (2)
Grandchildren

Vocation
Teaching Pastor,
Church Planter/
Consultant,
Men's Kingdom
Builders Ministry

Marriage

*My
Future
Bagel*

Friends/Hobbies

Boards

Family
Son (college)
Adult married
children (2)
Grandchildren (5)
Brother
Extended family

Vocation
Teaching Pastor,
Church Planter/
Consultant,
Men's Kingdom
Builders Ministry

Marriage
New Season
of Life

Insights for me:

Friends: I realized that I had many acquaintances but needed to give more time to developing quality relationships. God led me to capture more time with my friends by including them in my hobbies of hunting and golf. He showed me I needed to share my life more openly and be a better friend myself if I was going to enjoy meaningful friendships.

Family: Another insight He made known was that I needed to think more about being a leader in the lives of my aging mother-in-law and my grandchildren, which would require the reshaping of some of my time.

Marriage: Finally, this exercise prompted me to focus some getaway time with Carolyn to discuss and envision our future and new season of life together. Sharing these observations with Carolyn was meaningful to her because I had to be vulnerable and open to do so. It told her what I was processing on the inside about these God-given opportunities. More importantly, my sharing communicated that I valued taking responsibility for family relationships and people's lives, a value that is dear to her heart.

So, enjoy your bagel!

His Bagel

Now it's your turn. The bagel diagram below represents your mission in life. Two copies of this exercise are included for you and your wife to complete individually.

My Present Bagel

Step 1: Divide the bagel into sections indicating areas of opportunity or responsibility in your life. As you do this, consider how these areas may reveal the person of Jesus Christ. These could include marriage, family, vocation, friendships, hobbies, commitment at church, community service projects, etc. The size of each section should reflect the approximate percentage of time you devote to each. Your first pass should reflect your present bagel.

Step 2: Review the bagel you have just completed. Would your wife agree with the approximate percentages of times you have given to each area? Do you feel good about the order of your priorities and amount of time? What, if anything, do you want to change in the future? How might you better reflect the person of Jesus Christ?

Step 3: Now, complete your second bagel with any adjustments you believe need to be made. This one is labeled "My Future Bagel," indicating the way you want to use your time.

My Future Bagel

STEP 4: When you and your wife are finished, come together and share any discovery that the Lord revealed to you.

Getaway Verse

Whatever you do in word or deed, do all in the name of the Lord Jesus, giving thanks through Him to God the Father.

—Colossians 3:17

Getting Away <u>to Get It</u> Together

Her Bagel

Now it's your turn. The bagel diagram below represents your mission in life. Two copies of this exercise are included for you and your husband to complete individually.

My Present Bagel

Step 1: Divide the bagel into sections indicating areas of opportunity or responsibility in your life. As you do this, consider how these areas may reveal the person of Jesus Christ. These could include marriage, family, vocation, friendships, hobbies, commitment at church, community service projects, etc. The size of each section should reflect the approximate percentage of time you devote to each. Your first pass should reflect your present bagel.

Step 2: Review the bagel you have just completed. Would your husband agree with the approximate percentages of times you have given to each area? Do you feel good about the order of your priorities and amount of time? What, if anything, do you want to change in the future? How might you better reflect the person of Jesus Christ?

Step 3: Now, complete your second bagel with any adjustments you believe need to be made. This one is labeled "My Future Bagel," indicating the way you want to use your time.

My Future Bagel

STEP 4: When you and your husband are finished, come together and share any discovery that the Lord revealed to you.

Getaway Verse

Whatever you do in word or deed, do all in the name of the Lord Jesus, giving thanks through Him to God the Father.

—Colossians 3:17

Getting Away <u>to Get It</u> Together

His Bagel

Now it's your turn. The bagel diagram below represents your mission in life. Two copies of this exercise are included for you and your wife to complete individually.

My Present Bagel

Step 1: Divide the bagel into sections indicating areas of opportunity or responsibility in your life. As you do this, consider how these areas may reveal the person of Jesus Christ. These could include marriage, family, vocation, friendships, hobbies, commitment at church, community service projects, etc. The size of each section should reflect the approximate percentage of time you devote to each. Your first pass should reflect your present bagel.

Step 2: Review the bagel you have just completed. Would your wife agree with the approximate percentages of times you have given to each area? Do you feel good about the order of your priorities and amount of time? What, if anything, do you want to change in the future? How might you better reflect the person of Jesus Christ?

Step 3: Now, complete your second bagel with any adjustments you believe need to be made. This one is labeled "My Future Bagel," indicating the way you want to use your time.

My Future Bagel

STEP 4: When you and your wife are finished, come together and share any discovery that the Lord revealed to you.

Getaway Verse

Whatever you do in word or deed, do all in the name of the Lord Jesus, giving thanks through Him to God the Father.

—Colossians 3:17

Her Bagel

Now it's your turn. The bagel diagram below represents your mission in life. Two copies of this exercise are included for you and your husband to complete individually.

My Present Bagel

Step 1: Divide the bagel into sections indicating areas of opportunity or responsibility in your life. As you do this, consider how these areas may reveal the person of Jesus Christ. These could include marriage, family, vocation, friendships, hobbies, commitment at church, community service projects, etc. The size of each section should reflect the approximate percentage of time you devote to each. Your first pass should reflect your present bagel.

Step 2: Review the bagel you have just completed. Would your husband agree with the approximate percentages of times you have given to each area? Do you feel good about the order of your priorities and amount of time? What, if anything, do you want to change in the future? How might you better reflect the person of Jesus Christ?

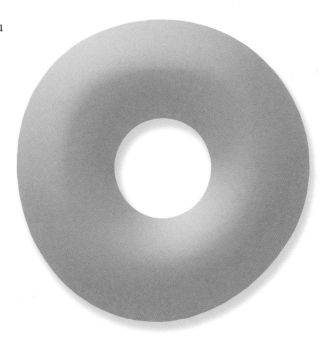

Step 3: Now, complete your second bagel with any adjustments you believe need to be made. This one is labeled "My Future Bagel," indicating the way you want to use your time.

My Future Bagel

STEP 4: When you and your husband are finished, come together and share any discovery that the Lord revealed to you.

Getaway Verse

Whatever you do in word or deed, do all in the name of the Lord Jesus, giving thanks through Him to God the Father.

—Colossians 3:17

Getting Away <u>to Get It</u> Together

Your Unique Design©
Discovering and living in your giftedness

David writes in Psalm 139 the following description of God's intimate involvement in crafting our one-of-a-kind design.

> *For You formed my inward parts; You wove me in my mother's womb. I will give thanks to You, for I am fearfully and wonderfully made; wonderful are Your works, and my soul knows it very well. My frame was not hidden from You, when I was made in secret, and skillfully wrought in the depths of the earth; your eyes have seen my unformed substance; and in Your book were all written the days that were ordained for me, when as yet there was not one of them.*
> —Psalm 139:13-16

The purpose of this exercise is to help you better understand your God-given design and what energizes you. This project will assist you in identifying your special talents and abilities. It will promote a couple's understanding of each other's designs and what you bring to each other in your marriage.

Step 1: Complete the Servants by Design™ Inventory at www.youruniquedesign.com and receive your personalized Profile Report prior to your getaway. This will be e-mailed to you within twenty-four hours of completing your inventory online.

Step 2: Review your profile, highlighting insights in each major section.

Step 3: Finally, write a brief design statement that captures your essence. Reduce your design statement to a design word as illustrated on the next page.

Step 4: Share your profile highlights with each other to better understand your design distinctives. For fun, compare and discuss your design condominiums (you'll find these in your profile). Share your first attempts at writing a personal design statement and design word. Affirm each other for the way God has uniquely crafted you.

Date completed:

———————

Design Statement

God has uniquely designed me to use my organizational and relational abilities to accomplish significant tasks and to bring practical wisdom and encouragement to others.

Design Word

Builder

Now give this a try below.

His Design Statement

_____

_____

_____

_____

_____

_____

_____

His Design Word

_____

Getaway Verse

For we are His workmanship, created in Christ Jesus for good works, which God prepared beforehand so that we would walk in them.

—Ephesians 2:10

Design Statement

God has uniquely designed me to use my organizational and relational abilities to accomplish significant tasks and to bring practical wisdom and encouragement to others.

Design Word

Builder

Now give this a try below.

Her Design Statement

_____

_____

_____

_____

_____

_____

Her Design Word

_____

Getaway Verse

For we are His workmanship, created in Christ Jesus for good works, which God prepared beforehand so that we would walk in them.

—Ephesians 2:10

Date completed:

_____

Design Statement

> God has uniquely designed me to use my organizational and relational abilities to accomplish significant tasks and to bring practical wisdom and encouragement to others.

Design Word

> Builder

Now give this a try below.

His Design Statement

_____

_____

_____

_____

_____

_____

His Design Word

_____

Getaway Verse

For we are His workmanship, created in Christ Jesus for good works, which God prepared beforehand so that we would walk in them.

—Ephesians 2:10

Design Statement

God has uniquely designed me to use my organizational and relational abilities to accomplish significant tasks and to bring practical wisdom and encouragement to others.

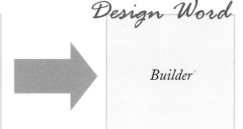

Design Word

Builder

Date completed:

_____

Now give this a try below.

Her Design Statement

_____

_____

_____

_____

_____

_____

Her Design Word

_____

Getaway Verse

For we are His workmanship, created in Christ Jesus for good works, which God prepared beforehand so that we would walk in them.

—Ephesians 2:10

Getting Away to Get It Together

Child Talk

Intentionality in training your young ones

from Carolyn

The child talk provides an opportunity for you to discuss each of your children's strengths and weaknesses in order to agree on a focus point for their training.

This is proactive parenting at its best! I love this project because it allows Bill and me to assess the progress of each of our children's development. It helps keep us unified in our parenting, increases our awareness of various issues and behavior patterns, and ultimately guides us in addressing the unique needs of each child.

To better see our children through each other's eyes, we separate and make notes on each child's strengths and weaknesses. We record some general observations and then come together again for discussion. We focus on one child at a time. While our insights overlap in many ways, occasionally one of us will illustrate a particular need or emerging trait in our child that the other has not recognized. This helps us agree on the best course of action for training our children.

I remember a time when one of our quieter children was being overshadowed in conversation around the dinner table. This child did not like to compete for time to talk and, as so often happens, "the squeaky wheel gets the grease." So as we discussed this issue on our getaway that year, Bill and I determined to make a special effort to draw her out during meal

We always conclude our child talk by praying together for God's blessing on each child, for the Lord to give them a heart for Him, and for wisdom in our parenting skills.

Now give it a try. The steps below are simple and rewarding.

Step 1: Individually, take a separate sheet of paper and write your child's name at the top. Divide the page into two columns. Label one "strengths" and the other "weaknesses." Develop one page for each child.

Step 2: Separately, write out what you believe are the strengths and weaknesses of each of your children. Also, record any general observations that you want to share.

Step 3: When you and your spouse are finished, come together and share your insights about each child.

Step 4: Finally, agree on one focus point for the training and encouragement of each child. Begin praying about these immediately. Talk about creative ways to build up your child in this area of need. Commit together to focus on this point for about six months and then re-evaluate. Remember, these are action steps you are taking as parents. This is not something for your child to do or even be aware of.

Getaway Verse

Train up a child in the way he should go, even when he is old he will not depart from it.

—Proverbs 22:6

Leaving a Legacy

Putting your family values on paper

from Bill

In Psalm 78, Asaph reminds us of the great importance of leaving a legacy from one generation to the next. Read his words carefully and observe the five generational impacts he describes.

> *For He established a testimony in Jacob and appointed a law in Israel, which He commanded our fathers that they should teach them to their children, that the generation to come might know, even the children yet to be born, that they may arise and tell them to their children, that they should put their confidence in God and not forget the works of God, but keep His commandments.*
>
> —Psalm 78:5-7

What values, truths, or principles would you like to pass on to your children and grandchildren? These lessons might come from success or failure, from a season of prosperity, or a time of pain. These could be about marriage, relationships, your walk with God, service to others, etc.

> *Carolyn and I have talked about our family values and worked hard at passing them on to our children. However, this is one project that I wish we had done from the outset of our child-rearing years. Having learned from experience, I am convinced it would have helped me be much more proactive and intentional about passing truth on to the next generation.*
>
> *On the next page I have listed a half-dozen of our values to stimulate your thinking.*

- We believe that marriage is a lifelong partnership between a man and a woman in total submission to God's authority (Genesis 1:26-28, 2:18-25, Ephesians 5:21-33, 1 Peter 3:1-7).

- We believe that children are a gift and special assignment from the Lord.

- We believe that each child has a unique set of design abilities and talents, and that we must help them discover these and encourage them to employ their God-given skills in a manner that glorifies Jesus Christ (Proverbs 22:6, Psalm 139:13-16).

- We believe in a work ethic that honors Jesus Christ as employer in daily thoughts, attitudes, and actions toward people and tasks (Ephesians 6:5-9, Colossians 3:22-4:1).

- We believe in spiritual integrity: that is, a consistency and growing harmony between our proclamation of God's Word and our incarnation of it (Psalm 15:1-2, Proverbs 11:3, James 1:22-25).

- We believe that we are to forgive others the way we have been forgiven by Jesus Christ (Matthew 6:14-15, Ephesians 4:31-32, Colossians 2:13).

- We believe that prayer is our best offense in every situation (Ephesians 6:18, Colossians 4:2-3, 1 Thessalonians 5:17-18, James 5:16).

Now, it's your opportunity to identify your family values to pass on to your children, family members, and even friends. Use the three simple steps below as your guide.

Step 1: Together, list the first six values you want to pass on in the space provided on the next two pages. Don't worry about exact wording at this point. Just list the values you want to represent the legacy of your life.

Step 2: Write down a passage of Scripture that supports each value.

Step 3: Look for windows of opportunity to share these values and biblical truths with your children and grandchildren. You might even want to develop a covenant or statement of your values to give to your family members.

Our Family Values

❀ _____

_____

_____

❀ _____

_____

_____

❀ _____

_____

_____

❀ _____

_____

_____

Getaway Verse

Unless the Lord builds the house, they labor in vain who build it; unless the Lord guards the city, the watchman keeps awake in vain.

—Psalm 127:1

Our Family Values

Date completed:

_____

✤ _____

_____

_____

✤ _____

_____

_____

✤ _____

_____

_____

✤ _____

_____

_____

Getaway Verse

Unless the Lord builds the house, they labor in vain who build it; unless the Lord guards the city, the watchman keeps awake in vain.

—Psalm 127:1

Financially Faithful

Investing in blessing

In 2 Corinthians 9:6-7, the apostle Paul exhorts us about giving to others out of the resources that God has given to us. He says, "Now this I say, he who sows sparingly will also reap sparingly, and he who sows bountifully will also reap bountifully. Each one must do just as he has purposed in his heart, not grudgingly or under compulsion, for God loves a cheerful giver."

Because there are so many worthy financial appeals, we are often challenged in deciding where to direct our support. This exercise will assist you as a couple in determining your financial investment toward meeting the needs of others.

Step 1: Together, make a list of the kinds of causes and needs you and your spouse are passionate about. For example, these could include opportunities like your church, marriage and family issues, discipleship, widows and orphans, disease, poverty, hunger, evangelism, etc. Keep in mind Paul's admonition in Galatians 6:6 as you do this: "The one who is taught the word is to share all good things with the one who teaches him." Very simply, be sure to give financially to those who give to you spiritually.

Step 2: Agree on the percentage of your income you believe the Lord would have you give. If you are not sure where to start, may I encourage you to use ten percent as a good rule of thumb. Of course, giving more with cheerfulness will mean greater blessings for you. List the annual/monthly amount God leads you to give in the Financially Faithful Worksheet that follows.

Step 3: Use the chart on the following page to list all your opportunities to give (Who?) and the reasons to do so (Why?). Is there agreement between your passions and purposes and those requesting your gifts? Where there is harmony, ask the Lord to unify your hearts, confirm your decision, and agree on the amount. If there is not harmony, say no to the opportunity until the Lord impresses you otherwise.

Step 4: Together, review your giving on an annual basis. Evaluate the measurable spiritual results of your giving in each area. Under God's direction, use the annual review as a time to decide to stop giving in some cases, recommit to others, and redirect your resources to new opportunities to give that fit your heart.

Getaway Verse

"In everything I showed you that by working hard in this manner you must help the weak and remember the words of the Lord Jesus, that He Himself said, 'It is more blessed to give than to receive.'"

—Acts 20:35

Financially Faithful Worksheet

Date completed:

_____

List below the amount you plan to give annually and monthly.

$_____/_____
        Annually   Monthly

Who?	Why?	Amount?
This column is to record the name of the ministry or person with financial need.	This column explains the cause or need that will be met because of your giving.	This column communicates the amount God leads you as a couple to invest.

Financially Faithful Worksheet

List below the amount you plan to give annually and monthly.

$_____ / _____

Annually   Monthly

Who?	Why?	Amount?
This column is to record the name of the ministry or person with financial need.	This column explains the cause or need that will be met because of your giving.	This column communicates the amount God leads you as a couple to invest.

Most-Wanted List

Bringing others along in your walk with God

In 1 Peter 3:15, the apostle Peter commands us: "Sanctify Christ as Lord in your hearts, always being ready to make a defense to everyone who asks you to give an account for the hope that is in you, yet with gentleness and reverence."

This exercise guides you to identify a Most-Wanted List of those you are fairly certain do not know Jesus Christ personally. It also challenges you to be prepared in advance "to give an account for the hope that is in you." Two copies of this exercise are included for you and your spouse to complete on your own. Share your responses with each other when you are finished.

Step 1: Ask God to reveal names of people to you that you are reasonably sure are not Christ followers. These might include a neighbor, an old friend, a co-worker, a family member, an acquaintance at the athletic club, a person you see at the barber shop or beauty salon, auto repair shop, grocery store, etc. God may even surprise you with a completely unexpected "divine appointment."

Step 2: Write three to five names on your Most-Wanted List. If you don't know the name, write a short description of the person and seek to find out their name after your getaway.

Step 3: Think about what circumstances brought you into a relationship with God and how the gospel has transformed your life. Jot down how you might share that with others on your Most-Wanted List. This message could include an outline that helps you move through a discussion point to point, a diagram that you sketch on a napkin, a written statement that helps you refine your thoughts, or some other creative method. There are many evangelistic tools, tracts, and methods to help, so choose one that fits you. Then memorize this presentation.

Step 4: Ask God to arrange these divine appointments. Be alert in conversation to special windows of opportunity to turn the discussion to spiritual things. As with the other projects, these sheets are duplicated here, providing his and her sets.

Sharing Christ with FORM

Years ago, Ron Blue, a professor from Dallas Seminary, shared this acrostic with me as an easy-to-remember way to direct a conversation toward sharing my testimony. It's the word FORM:

F . . . . . Tell me about your FAMILY or your family life growing up.

O . . . . . What do you do for a living? Or what do you enjoy most about your OCCUPATION?

R . . . . . Tell me about your RELIGIOUS background.

M . . . . Would you mind if I told you about mine? Share your prepared MESSAGE

His Most-Wanted List

_____

Step 5: Share your thoughts and action steps with each other.

Tell other believers what you are trusting God for with regard to sharing your testimony. Encourage them to do the same. If every Christ-follower would commit to share his faith just one time a year, it would be the greatest evangelistic outreach ever!

Getaway Verse

"Go therefore and make disciples of all the nations, baptizing them in the name of the Father and the Son and the Holy Spirit, teaching them to observe all that I commanded you; and lo, I am with you always, even to the end of the age."
—Matthew 28:19-20

Her Most-Wanted List

_____

_____

_____

_____

Step 5: Share your thoughts and action steps with each other.

Tell other believers what you are trusting God for with regard to sharing your testimony. Encourage them to do the same. If every Christ-follower would commit to share his faith just one time a year, it would be the greatest evangelistic outreach ever!

Getaway Verse

"Go therefore and make disciples of all the nations, baptizing them in the name of the Father and the Son and the Holy Spirit, teaching them to observe all that I commanded you; and lo, I am with you always, even to the end of the age."
—Matthew 28:19-20

His Most-Wanted List

_____

_____

_____

_____

_____

Step 5: Share your thoughts and action steps with each other.

Tell other believers what you are trusting God for with regard to sharing your testimony. Encourage them to do the same. If every Christ-follower would commit to share his faith just one time a year, it would be the greatest evangelistic outreach ever!

Getaway Verse

"Go therefore and make disciples of all the nations, baptizing them in the name of the Father and the Son and the Holy Spirit, teaching them to observe all that I commanded you; and lo, I am with you always, even to the end of the age."
—Matthew 28:19-20

Her Most-Wanted List

_____

_____

_____

_____

_____

Date completed:

_____

Step 5: Share your thoughts and action steps with each other.

Tell other believers what you are trusting God for with regard to sharing your testimony. Encourage them to do the same. If every Christ-follower would commit to share his faith just one time a year, it would be the greatest evangelistic outreach ever!

Getaway Verse

"Go therefore and make disciples of all the nations, baptizing them in the name of the Father and the Son and the Holy Spirit, teaching them to observe all that I commanded you; and lo, I am with you always, even to the end of the age."
—Matthew 28:19-20

His Most-Wanted List

_____

_____

_____

_____

_____

_____

Step 5: Share your thoughts and action steps with each other.

Tell other believers what you are trusting God for with regard to sharing your testimony. Encourage them to do the same. If every Christ-follower would commit to share his faith just one time a year, it would be the greatest evangelistic outreach ever!

Getaway Verse

"Go therefore and make disciples of all the nations, baptizing them in the name of the Father and the Son and the Holy Spirit, teaching them to observe all that I commanded you; and lo, I am with you always, even to the end of the age."
—Matthew 28:19-20

Her Most-Wanted List

Date completed:

_____

_____

_____

_____

_____

_____

Step 5: Share your thoughts and action steps with each other.

Tell other believers what you are trusting God for with regard to sharing your testimony. Encourage them to do the same. If every Christ-follower would commit to share his faith just one time a year, it would be the greatest evangelistic outreach ever!

Getaway Verse

"Go therefore and make disciples of all the nations, baptizing them in the name of the Father and the Son and the Holy Spirit, teaching them to observe all that I commanded you; and lo, I am with you always, even to the end of the age."
                              —Matthew 28:19-20

Getting Away _to Get It_ Together

Part Three

Getaway Takeaways

Date completed:

_____

Making the most of your marital investment

Before you start packing your bags to return home, there are three Getaway Takeaways designed to conclude your experience. His-and-her copies are provided for your responses. Your answers would be a great topic for conversation over lunch.

His Takeaway - Getaway 1

1. Write down and share what has been the most valuable aspect of your getaway experience. Explain why.

   _____

   _____

   _____

2. What do you understand are the most important steps of action you need to take? (You may want to quickly review the exercises you covered for this answer.)

   _____

   _____

3. When will you have your next getaway experience? Date: _____
   Be sure to mark your next getaway date on your calendar and your wife's calendar before leaving.

Her Takeaway - Getaway 1

1. Write down and share what has been the most valuable aspect of your getaway experience. Explain why.

_____

_____

_____

_____

2. What do you understand are the most important steps of action you need to take? (You may want to quickly review the exercises you covered for this answer.)

_____

_____

3. When will you have your next getaway experience? Date: _____
   Be sure to mark your next getaway date on your calendar and your husband's calendar before leaving.

Getaway Verse

"Why do you call Me, 'Lord, Lord,' and do not do what I say? Everyone who comes to Me and hears My words and acts on them, I will show you whom he is like: he is like a man building a house, who dug deep and laid a foundation on the rock; and when a flood occurred, the torrent burst against that house and could not shake it, because it had been well built. But the one who has heard and has not acted accordingly, is like a man who built a house on the ground without any foundation; and the torrent burst against it and immediately it collapsed, and the ruin of that house was great."

—Luke 6:46-49

His Takeaway - Getaway 2

1. Write down and share what has been the most valuable aspect of your getaway experience. Explain why.

   _____

   _____

   _____

2. What do you understand are the most important steps of action you need to take? (You may want to quickly review the exercises you covered for this answer.)

   _____

   _____

3. When will you have your next getaway experience? Date: _____
   Be sure to mark your next getaway date on your calendar and your wife's calendar before leaving.

Getaway Verse

"Why do you call Me, 'Lord, Lord,' and do not do what I say? Everyone who comes to Me and hears My words and acts on them, I will show you whom he is like: he is like a man building a house, who dug deep and laid a foundation on the rock; and when a flood occurred, the torrent burst against that house and could not shake it, because it had been well built. But the one who has heard and has not acted accordingly, is like a man who built a house on the ground without any foundation; and the torrent burst against it and immediately it collapsed, and the ruin of that house was great."
—Luke 6:46-49

Her Takeaway - Getaway 2

1. Write down and share what has been the most valuable aspect of your getaway experience. Explain why.

   _____

   _____

   _____

2. What do you understand are the most important steps of action you need to take? (You may want to quickly review the exercises you covered for this answer.)

   _____

   _____

3. When will you have your next getaway experience? Date: _____
   Be sure to mark your next getaway date on your calendar and your husband's calendar before leaving.

Getaway Verse

"Why do you call Me, 'Lord, Lord,' and do not do what I say? Everyone who comes to Me and hears My words and acts on them, I will show you whom he is like: he is like a man building a house, who dug deep and laid a foundation on the rock; and when a flood occurred, the torrent burst against that house and could not shake it, because it had been well built. But the one who has heard and has not acted accordingly, is like a man who built a house on the ground without any foundation; and the torrent burst against it and immediately it collapsed, and the ruin of that house was great."
                                                              —Luke 6:46-49

His Takeaway - Getaway 3

1. Write down and share what has been the most valuable aspect of your getaway experience. Explain why.

_____

_____

_____

2. What do you understand are the most important steps of action you need to take? (You may want to quickly review the exercises you covered for this answer.)

_____

_____

3. When will you have your next getaway experience? Date: _____
    Be sure to mark your next getaway date on your calendar and your wife's calendar before leaving.

Getaway Verse

"Why do you call Me, 'Lord, Lord,' and do not do what I say? Everyone who comes to Me and hears My words and acts on them, I will show you whom he is like: he is like a man building a house, who dug deep and laid a foundation on the rock; and when a flood occurred, the torrent burst against that house and could not shake it, because it had been well built. But the one who has heard and has not acted accordingly, is like a man who built a house on the ground without any foundation; and the torrent burst against it and immediately it collapsed, and the ruin of that house was great."
—Luke 6:46-49

Her Takeaway - Getaway 3

1. Write down and share what has been the most valuable aspect of your getaway experience. Explain why.

   _____

   _____

   _____

2. What do you understand are the most important steps of action you need to take? (You may want to quickly review the exercises you covered for this answer.)

   _____

   _____

3. When will you have your next getaway experience? Date: _____
   Be sure to mark your next getaway date on your calendar and your husband's calendar before leaving.

Getaway Verse

"Why do you call Me, 'Lord, Lord,' and do not do what I say? Everyone who comes to Me and hears My words and acts on them, I will show you whom he is like: he is like a man building a house, who dug deep and laid a foundation on the rock; and when a flood occurred, the torrent burst against that house and could not shake it, because it had been well built. But the one who has heard and has not acted accordingly, is like a man who built a house on the ground without any foundation; and the torrent burst against it and immediately it collapsed, and the ruin of that house was great."
                                                            —Luke 6:46-49

His Takeaway - Getaway 4

Date completed:

_____

1. Write down and share what has been the most valuable aspect of your getaway experience. Explain why.

_____

_____

_____

2. What do you understand are the most important steps of action you need to take? (You may want to quickly review the exercises you covered for this answer.)

_____

_____

3. When will you have your next getaway experience? Date: _____
   Be sure to mark your next getaway date on your calendar and your wife's calendar before leaving.

Getaway Verse

"Why do you call Me, 'Lord, Lord,' and do not do what I say? Everyone who comes to Me and hears My words and acts on them, I will show you whom he is like: he is like a man building a house, who dug deep and laid a foundation on the rock; and when a flood occurred, the torrent burst against that house and could not shake it, because it had been well built. But the one who has heard and has not acted accordingly, is like a man who built a house on the ground without any foundation; and the torrent burst against it and immediately it collapsed, and the ruin of that house was great."
                                                              —Luke 6:46-49

Her Takeaway - Getaway 4

1. Write down and share what has been the most valuable aspect of your getaway experience. Explain why.

_____

_____

_____

2. What do you understand are the most important steps of action you need to take? (You may want to quickly review the exercises you covered for this answer.)

_____

_____

3. When will you have your next getaway experience? Date: _____
   Be sure to mark your next getaway date on your calendar and your husband's calendar before leaving.

Getaway Verse

"Why do you call Me, 'Lord, Lord,' and do not do what I say? Everyone who comes to Me and hears My words and acts on them, I will show you whom he is like: he is like a man building a house, who dug deep and laid a foundation on the rock; and when a flood occurred, the torrent burst against that house and could not shake it, because it had been well built. But the one who has heard and has not acted accordingly, is like a man who built a house on the ground without any foundation; and the torrent burst against it and immediately it collapsed, and the ruin of that house was great."
—Luke 6:46-49

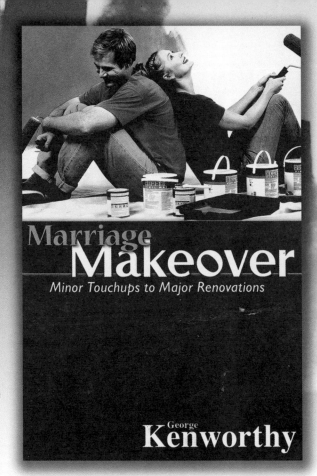